MW00848712

Five
Big Needle
Afghans

Created for Leisure Arts by House of White Birches

LEISURE
ARTS
the art of everyday living

Introduction

Nothing is better on a chilly winter night than wrapping up in a cozy, comfy afghan you've knit yourself. Here are five fantastic big-needle designs you can knit quickly for cool-weather comfort. Knit some for yourself and some to give away—everyone loves to be cuddled in afghans like these!

Table of Contents

Cozy & Warm Afghan 3

Diamonds Are for Cuddling 6

Fireside Comfort Afghan 10

Tiffany Afghan 13

Tuck-Me-In Afghan 16

Knitting Basics 18

Cozy & Warm Afghan

Design by Kathleen Power Johnson

Worked in one piece, this sumptuous afghan features an elementary lace pattern and a garter stitch border. Bulky weight yarn and large needles make this a perfect weekend project.

Skill Level ◼◼◻◻

EASY

Finished Size
Approx 58 x 60 inches

Materials
- Bulky weight wool yarn (78 yds/100g per ball): 14 balls ice blue
- Size 13 (9mm) 32- or 40-inch circular needle or size needed to obtain gauge

Gauge
11 sts and 16 rows = 4 inches/10cm in pat

To save time, take time to check gauge.

Special Abbreviation
Work 5 tog: Sl 2 sts knitwise, k1, pass 2 sl sts over k1, k2tog, pass first st over 2nd st.

Pattern Note
Circular needle is used to accommodate large number of stitches. Do not join at end of rows.

Afghan
Loosely cast on 127 sts. Knit 6 rows for border.

Row 1: K3, k2tog, *yo, k5, yo, sl 1, k2tog, psso; rep from * to last 10 sts, yo, k5, yo, ssk, k3.

Row 2 and all WS rows: K3, purl across to last st, end k3.

Rows 3 and 5: Rep Row 1.
Row 7: K3, *k1, yo, k1, yo, work 5 tog, yo, k1, yo; rep from * across to last 4 sts, end k4.
Row 9: K6, *yo, sl 1, k2tog, psso, yo, k5; rep from * across, end k1.
Rows 11 and 13: Rep Row 9.
Row 15: K3, k3tog, *yo, [k1, yo] 3 times, work 5 tog; rep from * to last 9 sts , yo, [k1, yo] 3 times, k3 tog, k3.
Row 16: Rep Row 2.

Rep Rows 1–16 until afghan measures approx 58 inches, ending with Row 15.

Knit 6 rows.

Bind off. Block lightly. ■

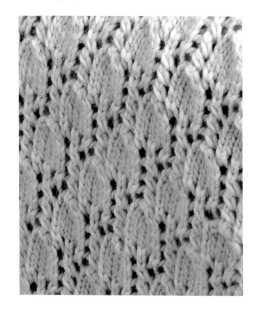

Diamonds
Are for Cuddling

Design by Kathleen Power Johnson

Made with chunky yarn, this quickie afghan features a captivating diamond stitch pattern and has a definite touch of class!

Skill Level
INTERMEDIATE

Finished Size
Approx 51 x 60 inches

Materials
- Super bulky yarn (64 yds/100g per ball): 20 balls cream

SUPER BULKY
- Size 15 (10mm) 29-inch circular needle or size needed to obtain gauge
- Size K/10½ (6.5mm) crochet hook (for fringe)

Gauge
8 sts and 12 rows = 4 inches/ 10cm in St st

To save time, take time to check gauge.

Pattern Note
Always knit first and last st of every row (edge sts).

Afghan
Loosely cast on 102 sts.

Knit 2 rows. Work in St st (knit 1 row, purl 1 row) for 4 inches.

Beg pat
Row 1 (RS): K3, *k1, [yo, ssk] 5 times, k1; rep from *, end k3.
Row 2 and all WS rows: K1, purl to last st, k1.
Row 3: K3, *k2, [yo, ssk] 4 times, k2; rep from * to last 3 sts, end k3.
Row 5: K6, [yo, ssk] 3 times, k2, yo, *ssk, k2, [yo, ssk] 3

times, k2, yo; rep from * to last 4 sts, end ssk, k2.

Row 7: K3, *yo, ssk, k2, [yo, ssk] twice, k2, yo, ssk; rep from * to last 3 sts, end k3.

Row 9: K2, [k2, yo, ssk] 3 times, yo, *ssk, [yo, ssk, k2] twice, yo, ssk, yo; rep from * to last 4 sts, end ssk, k2.

Row 11: K3, * [yo, ssk] twice, k4, [yo, ssk] twice; rep from * to last 3 sts, end k3.

Row 13: K4, [yo, ssk] twice, k2, [yo, ssk] twice, yo, *[ssk, yo] twice, ssk, k2, [yo, ssk] twice, yo; rep from * to last 4 sts, end ssk, k2.

Row 15: Rep Row 11.

Row 17: Rep Row 9.

Row 19: Rep Row 7.

Row 21: Rep Row 5.

Row 23: Rep Row 3.

Row 24: K1, purl to last st, k1.

Rep Rows 1–24 until afghan measures approx 52 inches, ending with Row 24.

Beg with a knit row, work in St st for 3½ inches, ending with a RS row. Knit 2 rows.

Bind off all sts.

Fringe

Make spaghetti fringe referring to page 9. For each short edge, cut 51 (17-inch) lengths of yarn. Use one strand for each knot. Tie knot in every other st of purl ridge across each short end. Trim ends even. ■

Rep

DIAMONDS AFGHAN CHART
Note: Only RS rows are shown

STITCH KEY
☐ Knit
⊙ Yo
◺ Ssk

Fringe

Cut a piece of cardboard half as long as specified in instructions for strands plus ½ inch for trimming. Wind yarn loosely and evenly around cardboard. When cardboard is filled, cut yarn across one end. Do this several times then begin fringing. Wind additional strands as necessary.

Single Knot Fringe

Hold specified number of strands for one knot together, fold in half. Hold project to be fringed with right side facing you. Use crochet hook to draw folded end through space or stitch indicated from right to wrong side.

Pull loose ends through folded section. Draw knot up firmly. Space knots as indicated in pattern instructions.

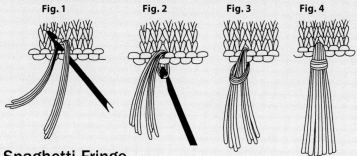

| Fig. 1 | Fig. 2 | Fig. 3 | Fig. 4 |

Spaghetti Fringe

Following Single Knot Fringe instructions, tie each knot with just one strand of yarn.

Fireside
Comfort Afghan

Design by Frances Hughes

Even when the cool air is nipping at your toes, you'll have this afghan to keep you warm. Choose three colors of worsted weight yarn for your own tweed look.

Skill Level

BEGINNER

Finished Size

Approx 52 x 60 inches

Materials

- Worsted weight yarn (228 yds/100g per skein): 5 skeins red (A), 5 skeins blue (B)
- Worsted weight yarn (260 yds/100g per skein): 10 skeins variegated red/blue (C)
- Size 17 (12.75mm) circular needle
- Size P/15/10mm crochet hook

Gauge

8 sts and 12 rows = 4 inches/ 10cm in St st with 4 strands held tog
To save time, take time to check gauge.

Afghan

Holding 1 strand each of A and B, and 2 strands C tog throughout, cast on 75 sts.

Rows 1–3: K1, *p1, k1; rep from * across.

Row 4: K1, p1, k1, knit to last 3 sts, k1, p1, k1.

Row 5: K1, p1, k1, purl to last 3 sts, k1, p1, k1.

Rows 6–23: [Rep Rows 4 and 5] 9 times.

Rows 24–45: [Rep Row 1] 22 times.

Rows 46–55: [Rep Rows 4 and 5] 5 times.

Rows 56–59: Rep Rows 1–4.

Row 60: K1, p1, k1, [k9, p3] 5 times, k9, k1, p1, k1.

Row 61: K1, p1, k1, [p9, k3] 5 times, p9, k1, p1, k1.

Rows 62–79: [Rep Rows 60 and 61] 9 times.

Rows 80–83: [Rep Row 1] 4 times.

Rows 84–93: [Rep Rows 4 and 5] 5 times.

Rows 94–115: [Rep Row 1] 22 times.

Rows 116–135: [Rep Rows 4 and 5] 10 times.

Rows 136–138: Rep Row 1. Bind off all sts.

Edging

Rnd 1: With 4 strands held tog and crochet hook, attach yarn with a sc in any st, *ch 4, sk next st, sc in next st; rep from * around; join with sl st in joining sc.

Rnds 2–4: Sl st in ch-4 sp, ch 1, sc in same sp, ch 4, *sc in next ch-4 sp, ch 4; rep from * around, join in first sc.

Fasten off. ∎

Tiffany
Afghan

Design by Kathleen Power Johnson

This warm and wonderful afghan is knit in classic colors of red and white with the variegated red providing jewel tones. You'll appreciate how quickly it works up in super bulky yarn and size 17 needles.

Skill Level   ◼◻◻◻
BEGINNER

Finished Size
Approx 45 x 55 inches

Materials
- Super bulky weight acrylic yarn (84 yds/140g per ball): 9 balls red variegated (MC)
- Super bulky weight acrylic blend yarn (108 yds/6 oz per ball): 3 balls fisherman (CC)
- Size 17 (12.75mm) 36-inch circular needle or size needed to obtain gauge

Gauge
8 sts and 10 rows = 4 inches/ 10cm in St st
To save time, take time to check gauge.

Pattern Note
Circular needle is used to accommodate large number of sts; work back and forth in rows, do not join.

Afghan
With MC, loosely cast on 85 sts. Knit 3 rows.
Row 1 (RS): With CC, k2, *sl 1 wyib, k3; rep from *, end sl 1, k2.

Row 2: With CC, p2, *sl 1 wyif, p3; rep from *, end sl 1, p2.
Row 3: With MC, k4, *sl 1 wyib, k3; rep from *, end sl 1, k4.
Row 4: With MC, p4, *sl 1 wyif, p3; rep from *, end sl 1, p4.
Rows 5 and 6: With MC, knit.
Row 7: With CC, k4, *sl 1 wyib, k3; rep from *, end sl 1, k4.
Row 8: With CC, p4, *sl 1 wyif, p3; rep from *, end sl 1, p4.
Row 9: With MC, k2, *sl 1 wyib, k3; rep from *, end sl 1, k2.
Row 10: With MC, p2, *sl 1 wyif, p3; rep from *, end sl 1, p2.
Rows 11 and 12: Knit.
Rep Rows 1–12 of pat until afghan measures approx 55 inches, ending with Row 6 or 12. Knit 1 row.
Bind off loosely.

Finishing

With RS facing, pick up and knit 104 sts along long edge.
Knit 3 rows.
Bind off all sts.
Rep for opposite side. ∎

Tuck-Me-in
Afghan

Design by Kathleen Power Johnson

The all-over tuck stitch of this luscious afghan creates the feel of a down comforter. Everyone in the family will want a knitted afghan to snuggle under at night.

Skill Level ◑■☐☐
EASY

Finished Size
Approximately 60 x 80 inches

Materials
- Bulky weight acrylic yarn (135 yds/85g per skein): 20 skeins lilac
- Size 11 (8mm) circular needle or size required to obtain gauge
- Tapestry needle

Gauge
11 sts and 24 rows = 4 inches/10cm in pat

To save time, take time to check gauge.
Note: Gauge is easier to measure on WS of pat.

Pattern Stitches
A. Ribbed Border
Row 1 (WS): K4, *p1, k2, rep from *, end k2.
Row 2: K2, p2, *k1, p2, rep from *, end k2.
Rep Rows 1 and 2 for pat.
B. Drop Stitch Pat (multiple of 3 sts + 2 + 4 selvage sts)
Rows 1, 3 and 5 (WS): K4, *p1, k2, rep from *, end k2.
Rows 2 and 4: K2, p2, *k1, p2, rep from *, end k2.

Row 6: K2, p2, *drop next st and unravel it down 4 rows, insert tip of RH needle knitwise into 5th st down and also under 4 loose strands and k1, drawing st up with strands behind it, p2, rep from *, end k2.
Rep Rows 1–6 for pat.

Afghan

Cast on 222 sts. Work Pat A for 2 inches, ending with a RS row. Work Pat B for approximately 58 inches, ending with Row 6. Work Pat A for 2 inches. Bind off all sts in pat. ■

Yarn Information

Each project in this leaflet was made using various weights of yarn. Any brand of specified weight of yarn may be used. It is best to refer to the yardage/meters when determining how many balls or skeins to purchase. Remember, to arrive at the finished size, it is the GAUGE/ TENSION that is important, not the brand of yarn. For your convenience, listed below are the specific yarns used to create our photography models.

Page 3: Cozy & Warm Afghan—Sample project was completed with UpCountry (100 percent wool) color #80953 ice blue from Patons Yarns.
Page 7: Diamonds Are for Cuddling—Sample project was completed with Encore Mega Chunky (75 percent arylic/25 percent wool) color #256 cream from Plymouth Yarn Inc.
Page 10: Fireside Comfort Afghan—Yarn information not available.
Page 13: Tiffany Afghan—Sample project was completed with Jiffy Thick & Quick (100 percent acrylic) color #210 Ozarks (MC) and Wool-Ease Thick & Quick (80 percent acrylic/20 percent wool) color #099 fisherman (CC) from Lion Brand Yarn Co.
Page 16: Tuck-Me-in Afghan—Sample project was completed with Jiffy (100 percent acrylic) color #144 lilac from Lion Brand Yarn Co.

Knitting Basics

Skill Levels

BEGINNER
Projects for first-time knitters using basic knit and purl stitches. Minimal shaping.

EASY
Projects using basic stitches, repetitive stitch patterns, simple color changes and simple shaping and finishing.

INTERMEDIATE
Projects with a variety of stitches, such as basic cables and lace, simple intarsia, double-pointed needles and knitting in the round needle techniques, mid-level shaping and finishing.

EXPERIENCED
Projects using advanced techniques and stitches, such as short rows, Fair Isle, more intricate intarsia, cables, lace patterns and numerous color changes.

Standard Abbreviations

[ ] work instructions within brackets as many times as directed

( ) work instructions within parentheses in the place directed

** repeat instructions following the asterisks as directed

* repeat instructions following the single asterisk as directed

" inch(es)

approx approximately

beg begin/beginning

CC contrasting color

ch chain stitch

cm centimeter(s)

cn cable needle

dec decrease/decreases/decreasing

dpn(s) double-pointed needle(s)

g gram

inc increase/increases/increasing

k knit

k2tog knit 2 stitches together

LH left hand

lp(s) loop(s)

m meter(s)

M1 make one stitch

MC main color

mm millimeter(s)

oz ounce(s)

p purl

pat(s) pattern(s)

p2tog purl 2 stitches together

psso pass slipped stitch over

rem remain/remaining

rep repeat(s)

rev St st reverse stockinette stitch

RH right hand

rnd(s) rounds

RS right side

sc single crochet

skp slip, knit, pass stitch over—one stitch decreased

sk2p slip 1, knit 2 together, pass slip stitch over the knit 2 together; 2 stitches have been decreased

sl slip

sl 1k slip 1 knitwise

sl 1p slip 1 purlwise

sl st slip stitch(es)

ssk slip, slip, knit these 2 stitches together—a decrease

sp space

st(s) stitch(es)

St st stockinette stitch/stocking stitch

tbl through back loop(s)

tog together

WS wrong side

wyib with yarn in back

wyif with yarn in front

yd(s) yard(s)

yfwd yarn forward

yo yarn over

Cast On

Leaving an end about an inch long for each stitch to be cast on, make a slip knot on the right needle.

Place the thumb and index finger of your left hand between the yarn ends with the long yarn end over your thumb, and the strand from the skein over your index finger. Close your other fingers over the strands to hold them against your palm. Spread your thumb and index fingers apart and draw the yarn into a "V."

Place the needle in front of the strand around your thumb and bring it underneath this strand. Carry the needle over and under the strand on your index finger.

Draw through loop on thumb.

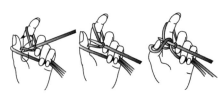

Drop the loop from your thumb and draw up the strand to form a stitch on the needle.

Repeat until you have cast on the number of stitches indicated in the pattern. Remember to count the beginning slip knot as a stitch.

Cable Cast On

This type of cast on is used when adding stitches in the middle or at the end of a row.

Make a slip knot on the left needle.

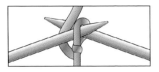

Knit a stitch in this knot and place it on the left needle.

Insert the right needle between the last two stitches on the left needle. Knit a stitch and place it on the left needle. Repeat for each stitch needed.

Knit (k)

Insert tip of right needle from front to back in next stitch on left needle.

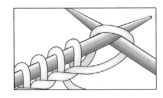

Bring yarn under and over the tip of the right needle.

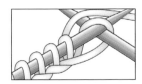

Pull yarn loop through the stitch with right needle point.

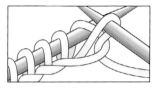

Slide the stitch off the left needle. The new stitch is on the right needle.

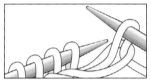

Purl (p)

With yarn in front, insert tip of right needle from back to front through next stitch on the left needle.

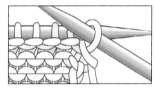

Bring yarn around the right needle counterclockwise.

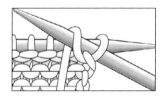

With right needle, draw yarn back through the stitch.

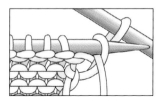

Slide the stitch off the left needle. The new stitch is on the right needle.

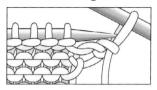

Bind Off
Binding off (knit)

Knit first two stitches on left needle. Insert tip of left needle into first stitch worked on right needle and pull it over the second stitch and completely off the needle.

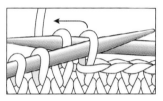

Knit the next stitch and repeat. When one stitch remains on right needle, cut yarn and draw tail through last stitch to fasten off.

Binding off (purl)

Purl first two stitches on left needle. Insert tip of left needle into first stitch worked on right needle and pull it over the second stitch and completely off the needle.

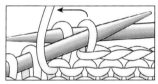

Purl the next stitch and repeat. When one stitch remains on right needle, cut yarn and draw tail through last stitch to fasten off.

Increase (inc)

Two stitches in one stitch Increase (knit)

Knit the next stitch in the usual manner, but don't remove the stitch from the left needle. Place right needle behind left needle and knit again into the back of the same stitch. Slip original stitch off left needle.

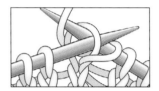

Increase (purl)

Purl the next stitch in the usual manner, but don't remove the stitch from the left needle. Place right needle behind left needle and purl again into the back of the same stitch. Slip original stitch off left needle.

Invisible Increase (M1)

There are several ways to make or increase one stitch.

Make 1 with Left Twist (M1L)

Insert left needle from front to back under the horizontal loop between the last stitch worked and next stitch on left needle.

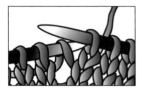

With right needle, knit into the back of this loop.

To make this increase on the purl side, insert left needle in same manner and purl into the back of the loop.

Make 1 with Right Twist (M1R)

Insert left needle from back to front under the horizontal loop between the last stitch worked and next stitch on left needle.

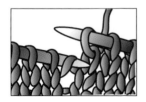

With right needle, knit into the front of this loop.

To make this increase on the purl side, insert left needle in same manner and purl into the front of the loop.

Make 1 with Backward Loop over the right needle

With your thumb, make a loop over the right needle.

Slip the loop from your thumb onto the needle and pull to tighten.

Make 1 in top of stitch below

Insert tip of right needle into the stitch on left needle one row below.

Knit this stitch, then knit the stitch on the left needle.

Decrease (dec)

Knit 2 together (k2tog)

Put tip of right needle through next two stitches on left needle as to knit. Knit these two stitches as one.

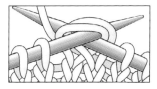

Purl 2 together (p2tog)

Put tip of right needle through next two stitches on left needle as to purl. Purl these two stitches as one.

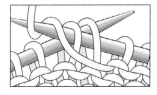

Slip, Slip, Knit (ssk)

Slip next two stitches, one at a time, as to knit from left needle to right needle.

Insert left needle in front of both stitches and work off needle together.

Slip, Slip, Purl (ssp)

Slip next two stitches, one at a time, as to knit from left needle to right needle. Slip these stitches back onto left needle keeping them twisted.

Purl these two stitches together through back loops.

Standard Yarn Weight System

Categories of yarn, gauge ranges, and recommended needle sizes

Yarn Weight Symbol & Category Names	1 SUPER FINE	2 FINE	3 LIGHT	4 MEDIUM	5 BULKY	6 SUPER BULKY
Type of Yarns in Category	Sock, Fingering, Baby	Sport, Baby	DK, Light Worsted	Worsted, Afghan, Aran	Chunky, Craft, Rug	Bulky, Roving
Knit Gauge* Ranges in Stockinette Stitch to 4 inches	21–32 sts	23–26 sts	21–24 sts	16–20 sts	12–15 sts	6–11 sts
Recommended Needle in Metric Size Range	2.25–3.25mm	3.25–3.75mm	3.75–4.5mm	4.5–5.5mm	5.5–8mm	8mm
Recommended Needle U.S. Size Range	1 to 3	3 to 5	5 to 7	7 to 9	9 to 11	11 and larger

* GUIDELINES ONLY: The above reflect the most commonly used gauges and needle sizes for specific yarn categori

Five Big Needle Afghans © 2005, 2004, 2003 House of White Birches, 306 East Parr Road, Berne, IN 46711, (260) 589-4000. Customer_Serviece@whitebirches.com. Made in USA.

This publication is protected under federal copyright laws. Reproduction or distribution of this publication or any other House of White Birches or Leisure Arts publication, including publications which are out of print, is prohibited unless specifically authorized. This includes, but is not limited to, any form of reproduction or distribution on or through the Internet, including posting, scanning or e-mail transmission.

We have made every effort to ensure that the instructions in this book are complete and accurate.
We cannot be responsible for human error, typographical mistakes or variations in individual work. The designs in this book are protected by copyright; however, you may make the designs for your personal use. This right is surpassed when the designs are made by employees or sold commercially.

Published by Leisure Arts, Inc., 104 Champs Blvd., Ste. 100, Maumelle, Arkansas 72113.

All rights reserved